WHEN DHRUVA SAW UTTAMA SITTING ON UTTANAPADA'S LAP, HE RAN TOWARDS THEM.

I TOO WILL SIT ON MY FATHER'S LAP.

CERTAINLY NOT!

YOU HAVE NO RIGHT TO BE THERE. GO AWAY.

WHERE SHALL I GO, MOTHER?

GO TO LORD NARAYANA* AND SEEK HIS FAVOUR TO BE REBORN AS MY SON. ONLY THEN CAN YOU ENJOY THE SAME RIGHTS AS UTTAMA.

* ANOTHER NAME FOR VISHNU.

2

STUNG BY HER WORDS, DHRUVA RAN CRYING TO HIS MOTHER.

WHY ARE YOU CRYING, DHRUVA? HAS ANYONE HURT YOU?

MOTHER SURUCHI SAID I HAD NO RIGHT TO SIT ON MY FATHER'S LAP.

SHE SAID ONLY UTTAMA HAD THE RIGHT TO SIT ON THE KING'S LAP.

SHE'S RIGHT, DHRUVA.

HOLDING BACK HER TEARS, SUNEETI HUGGED HIM AND CARRIED HIM IN.

I AM A KSHATRIYA PRINCE, AM I NOT, MOTHER?

YES, MY CHILD.

SECURE IN HIS MOTHER'S ARMS, DHRUVA BECAME CALM AND THOUGHTFUL.

MOTHER, SURUCHI TOLD ME TO GO AND SEEK LORD NARAYANA'S FAVOUR IF I WANT TO SIT ON MY FATHER'S LAP.

MEANWHILE, SAGE NARADA CAME TO KNOW ABOUT SURUCHI'S HARSH WORDS AND DHRUVA'S RESOLVE.

HE IS A TRUE KSHATRIYA INDEED. THOUGH A MERE CHILD, HE WILL NOT BROOK THE INSULTS OF HIS STEP-MOTHER. YET WHAT HE SEEKS IS IMPOSSIBLL. I MUST SPEAK TO HIM.

NARADA WENT TO SEE DHRUVA.

MY CHILD, WHY DON'T YOU ACCEPT YOUR FATE AND GO BACK TO YOUR MOTHER?

O MASTER, I AM DHRUVA, THE SON OF MIGHTY UTTANAPADA, A KSHATRIYA. AND I AM DETERMINED TO WIN THE LORD'S FAVOUR.

I AM AWARE OF THAT, MY CHILD. BUT YOU ARE TOO YOUNG. IT IS NOT EASY TO FIND LORD NARAYANA. WHY DON'T YOU WAIT TILL YOU ARE A LITTLE OLDER?

FORGIVE ME, MASTER, BUT I WILL NOT TURN BACK. O WISE ONE, TELL ME HOW I CAN SUCCEED IN MY RESOLVE.

NARADA WAS EXTREMELY PLEASED BY HIS DETERMINATION.

IF YOU MEDITATE IN THE MADHUVAN FOREST ON THE BANKS OF THE YAMUNA, YOU WILL FIND THE LORD.

O SAINT, TEACH ME HOW TO MEDITATE.

REPEAT WITH ME—
*OM NAMO BHAGAWATE VASUDEVAYA !

OM NAMO BHAGAWATE VASUDEVAYA.

SAY THAT OVER AND OVER AGAIN, AND CONCENTRATE ON THAT.

AS DHRUVA SET OUT FOR MADHUVAN, NARADA WENT TO THE PALACE OF KING UTTANAPADA.

WELCOME! WELCOME, SAGE NARADA. PLEASE BE SEATED.

NARADA NOTICED THAT THOUGH UTTANA-PADA WELCOMED HIM RESPECTFULLY, HIS MIND WAS ELSEWHERE.

O KING, WHAT ARE YOU THINKING ABOUT?

HOLY SAGE, I AM THE VILEST OF MEN. I DID NOT UTTER A WORD WHEN SURUCHI DROVE POOR DHRUVA AWAY WITH HER CRUEL WORDS.

ALAS! HE HAS GONE AWAY ALONE INTO THE FOREST. THE BEASTS WILL DEVOUR HIM.

FEAR NOT, O KING. THE LORD HIM-SELF WILL PROTECT YOUR SON. HE WILL COME BACK BRINGING GLORY TO ALL.

* BOW TO THE REVERED VASUDEVA (VISHNU).

MEANWHILE, DHRUVA HAD REACHED MADHUVAN.

I SHALL SIT HERE AND BEGIN MY MEDITATION.

IN THE FIRST MONTH, HE LIVED ONLY ON THE FRUITS HE COULD FIND IN THE FOREST.

GRADUALLY HE GAVE UP EVEN THAT AND ATE ONLY GRASS AND LEAVES.

IN THE THIRD MONTH, HE STOPPED EATING AND LIVED ONLY ON WATER.

IN THE FOURTH MONTH, HE GAVE UP EVEN THAT AND LIVED ON AIR. THROUGHOUT THE PERIOD HE REPEATED THE MANTRA OVER AND OVER AGAIN.

OM NAMO BHAGAVATE VASUDEVAYA!

IN THE FIFTH AND SIXTH MONTHS, HE EVEN STOPPED BREATHING.

OM NAMO BHAGAVATE VASUDEVAYA.

DHRUVA'S CONCENTRATION STOPPED THE VERY AIR FROM FLOWING. THERE WAS PANIC IN HEAVEN...

MEANWHILE, AS DHRUVA MEDITATED —

LORD, I THOUGHT I HAD FOUND YOU BUT YOU'VE SUDDENLY VANISHED. HAVE I FAILED IN MY WORSHIP? HAVE I DISPLEASED YOU? THEN I SHALL START MEDITATING ALL OVER AGAIN.

AND DHRUVA OPENED HIS EYES.

THE LORD HAS COME TO ME!

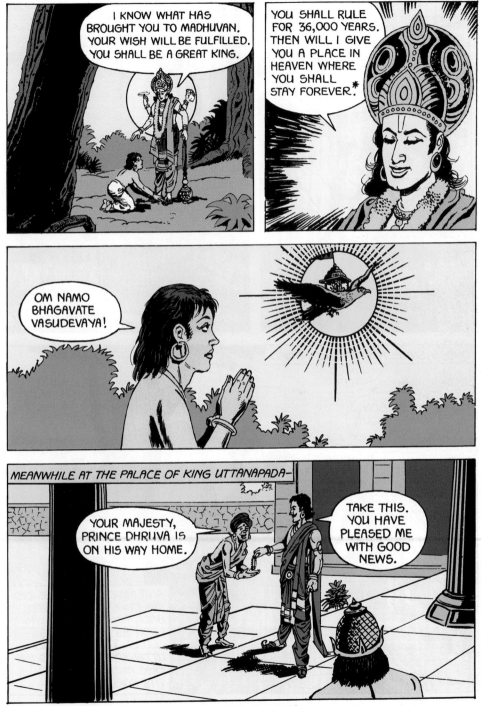

*THE POLE STAR TO THIS DAY IS KNOWN AS DHRUVA.

ASHTAVAKRA

KAHODA WAS THE FAVOURITE DISCIPLE OF UDDALAKA, A RENOWNED SCHOLAR IN THE VEDAS. UDDALAKA HAD A DAUGHTER CALLED SUJATA.

ONE DAY— I AM PLEASED WITH YOUR DEVOTION, KAHODA. AS SOON AS YOU HAVE MASTERED THE SACRED TEXTS...

...YOU SHALL HAVE MY DAUGHTER, SUJATA, FOR A WIFE

KAHODA WAS CLEVER AND HARD-WORKING AND SOON MASTERED THE TEXTS. AS HIS GURU HAD PROMISED HE WAS MARRIED TO SUJATA.

YOU MAY CONTINUE TO LIVE HERE AT THE ASHRAM, AND TEACH YOUR DISCIPLES.

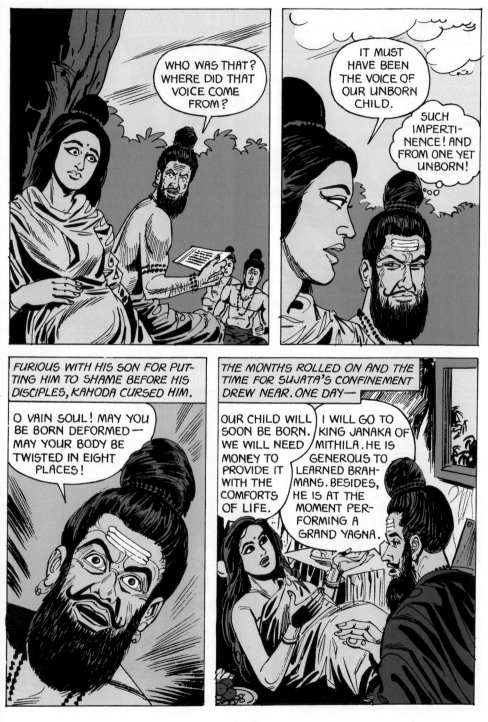

WHO WAS THAT? WHERE DID THAT VOICE COME FROM?

IT MUST HAVE BEEN THE VOICE OF OUR UNBORN CHILD.

SUCH IMPERTINENCE! AND FROM ONE YET UNBORN!

FURIOUS WITH HIS SON FOR PUTTING HIM TO SHAME BEFORE HIS DISCIPLES, KAHODA CURSED HIM.

O VAIN SOUL! MAY YOU BE BORN DEFORMED— MAY YOUR BODY BE TWISTED IN EIGHT PLACES!

THE MONTHS ROLLED ON AND THE TIME FOR SUJATA'S CONFINEMENT DREW NEAR. ONE DAY—

OUR CHILD WILL SOON BE BORN. WE WILL NEED MONEY TO PROVIDE IT WITH THE COMFORTS OF LIFE.

I WILL GO TO KING JANAKA OF MITHILA. HE IS GENEROUS TO LEARNED BRAHMANS. BESIDES, HE IS AT THE MOMENT PERFORMING A GRAND YAGNA.

THE DEBATE BEGAN BUT DID NOT CONTINUE FOR LONG. KAHODA WAS NO MATCH FOR BANDHI.

BANDHI HAS WON AGAIN. POOR KAHODA WILL BE DROWNED LIKE ALL THE OTHERS.

BANDHI WAS TRIUMPHANT.

MY MISSION HERE IS PROVING TO BE VERY SUCCESSFUL. I HAVE BEEN ABLE TO DISPATCH ONE MORE SAGE.

*CROOKED IN EIGHT PLACES.

...ASHTAVAKRA SOON BEGAN TO LOOK UPON HIM AS HIS FATHER.

THE YEARS ROLLED ON. UDDALAKA TAUGHT ASHTA-VAKRA AND SHWETAKETU.

WHEN THE BOYS WERE TWELVE YEARS OLD—

YOU HAVE MASTERED THE VEDAS. I AM PROUD OF YOU, MY SON.

AND SUJATA TOLD HIM ALL THAT HAD HAPPENED.

I MUST DEFEAT BANDHI AND HAVE HIM DROWNED.

THAT NIGHT—

COME ON, SHWETAKETU. LET US GO TO MITHILA. IT WILL BE A GOOD EXPERIENCE FOR US. KING JANAKA HAS NOT BEEN ABLE TO COMPLETE THE YAGNA HE STARTED TWELVE YEARS AGO.

SHWETAKETU WAS WILLING.

WHEN DO YOU WANT TO LEAVE?

AT ONCE.

22

THAT'S BECAUSE HE WAS NEVER CONFRONTED WITH A SCHOLAR OF MY CALIBRE. I WILL NOT GO BACK TILL I SEE HIM DEFEATED AND DROWNED.

WHEN JANAKA SAW THAT ASHTAVAKRA WAS ADAMANT—

THE BOY IS CONFIDENT. I WILL TEST HIS INTELLIGENCE. BY ASKING HIM A FEW QUESTIONS.

IF YOU CAN ANSWER MY QUESTIONS I WILL LET YOU MEET BANDHI.

WHAT IS IT THAT DOES NOT MOVE WHEN BORN?

AN EGG.

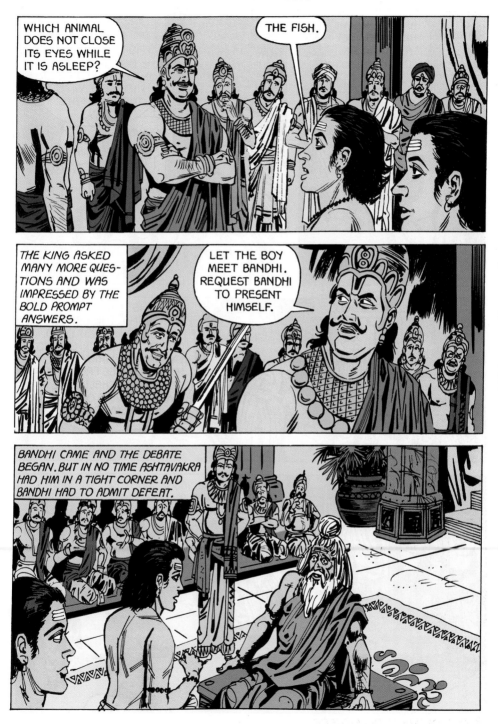

*LORD OF THE HYDROSPHERE.

NOW WITH YOUR PERMISSION, O KING, I WILL GO BACK TO MY FATHER'S KINGDOM.

THEN AS THEY WATCHED, BANDHI JUMPED INTO THE WATER...

KAHODA, ASHTAVAKRA AND SHWETAKETU RETURNED TO THE HERMITAGE. AS SOON AS THEY ARRIVED THERE, KAHODA TOOK SUJATA AND ASHTAVAKRA TO THE RIVER FLOWING NEAR BY.

ASHTAVAKRA, TAKE A QUICK PLUNGE INTO THE RIVER AND COME OUT.

TALES OF VISHNU

The route to your roots

TALES OF VISHNU

Vishnu, they say, is just one of a powerful threesome – the highest lords of the universe. However, though Brahma has created the universe and Shiva can destroy it, it is up to the great god Vishnu to keep all creatures within it well and happy. Always compassionate, he is also the wisest of the trinity. It is he who good-naturedly sorts out the mess the others create. And above all, Vishnu always favours the good and the pure.

Script
Subba Rao

Illustrations
H.S.Chavan

Editor
Anant Pai

INDRADYUMNA THEN RETIRED TO THE KULACHALA MOUNTAINS WHERE HE BUILT A COTTAGE FOR HIMSELF. OBSERVING THE VOW OF SILENCE, HE SAT WITH HIS MIND DWELLING UPON LORD VISHNU.

ONE DAY, SAGE AGASTYA CAME THAT WAY WITH HIS DISCIPLES.

WE HAVE COME TO HIS DOOR AND HE DOES NOT HAVE THE COURTESY TO WELCOME US!

YOUR ARROGANCE SHALL NOT GO UNPUNISHED! MAY YOU TURN INTO AN ELEPHANT.

INDRADYUMNA EASILY OVERPOWERED HIS RIVAL.

WE SALUTE YOU, O GAJENDRA*!

ONE DAY —

LET US GO TO THE TRIKUTA MOUNTAIN. IT'S A BETTER PLACE THAN THIS.

WE'LL FOLLOW YOU TO THE END OF THE EARTH, O GAJENDRA.

LED BY GAJENDRA, THE HERD TOOK THE TRIKUTA FOREST BY STORM.

*KING ELEPHANT

TRUMPETING LOUDLY, HE TRIED TO SHAKE OFF THE CROCODILE.

BUT ALL HIS EFFORTS WERE IN VAIN.

IT'S A CROCODILE. HE'S CAUGHT MY LEG.

WE'RE COMING, MY LORD. WE'LL SAVE YOU.

8

AMBARISHA

AFTER FASTING FOR THREE DAYS, KING AMBARISHA WORSHIPPED LORD VISHNU IN THE FOREST OF MADHUVANA*. HE WAS TO BREAK HIS FAST ON THE AUSPICIOUS DAY OF DWADASHI.✝

HAVING GIVEN AWAY ALMS...

...AND FED MENDICANTS...

*THE FOREST REGION AROUND MATHURA ✝THE TWELFTH DAY OF THE FORTNIGHT

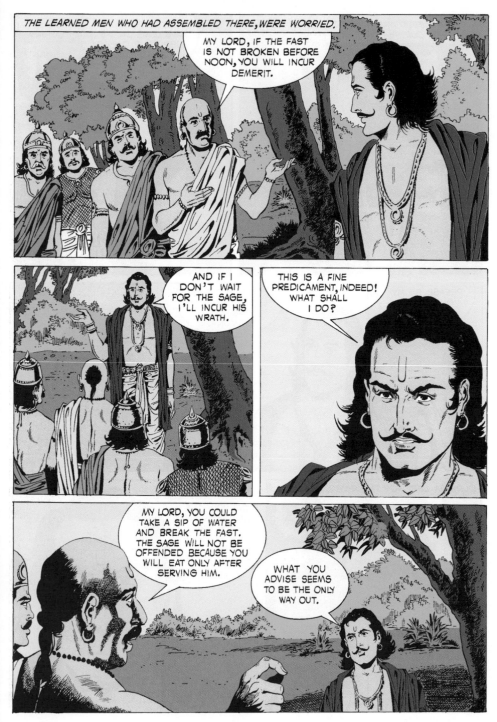

THE COURTIERS WERE AGHAST.

ISN'T THE SAGE AWARE OF THE CONDITIONS LAID DOWN FOR THE BREAKING OF THIS FAST?

WHY DID HE KEEP OUR KING WAITING?

DON'T WORRY. I THINK HE WILL SOON GET OVER HIS FIT OF RAGE.

BUT THE COURTIER WAS IN FOR A SHOCK. THE NEXT MOMENT—

YOU SHALL PAY FOR YOUR ARROGANCE, AMBARISHA!

THE SAGE TORE OFF A LOCK OF HIS MATTED HAIR.

AND LO! IT TURNED INTO A DISCUS.

HAVING DESTROYED THE DISCUS WHICH THREATENED AMBARISHA'S LIFE, SUDARSHANA CHAKRA FLEW TOWARDS DURVASA.

IT'S HEADING FOR ME!

THE SAGE BROKE INTO A RUN, PURSUED BY THE CHAKRA.

19

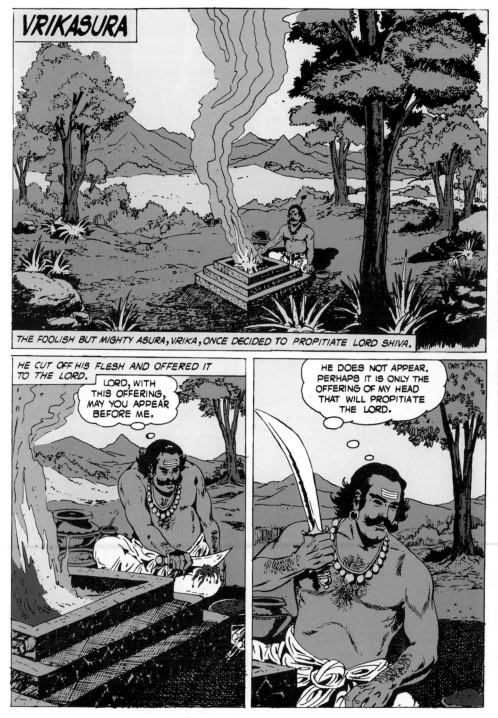

MEANWHILE, AS VRIKA RAN IN SEARCH OF SHIVA, A YOUNG BRAHMACHARI *MET HIM.

WHERE ARE YOU RUNNING TO? WHOM ARE YOU SEEKING? REST FOR A WHILE. YOU SEEM TIRED.

VRIKA TOLD HIM OF SHIVA'S BOON.

WHEN I WANTED TO TRY IT ON HIM, HE RAN AWAY.

THAT'S BECAUSE THE MOMENT YOU PLACED YOUR PALM ON HIS HEAD, YOU WOULD REALISE THAT HE HAD DUPED YOU.

WHAT! SHIVA DUPING A DEVOTEE! I CAN'T BELIEVE IT.

THEN WHY DON'T YOU PLACE YOUR PALM ON YOUR OWN HEAD AND SEE?

A GOOD IDEA!

*CELIBATE

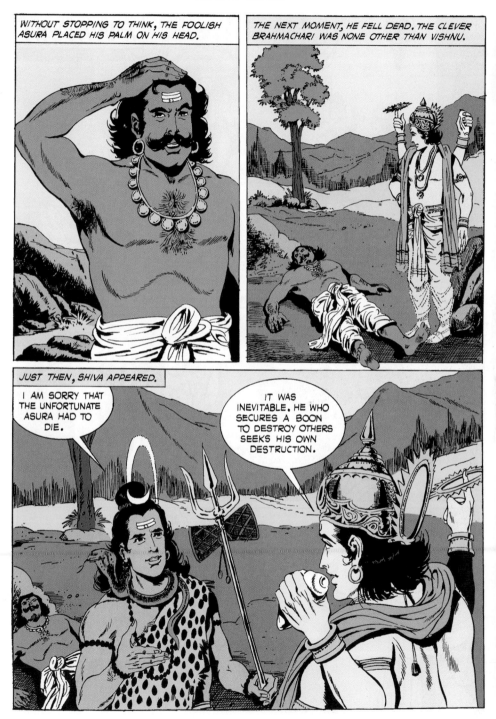

25

RANTIDEVA

ONCE BRAHMA, INDRA AND THE OTHER DEVAS CALLED ON LORD VISHNU.

LORD, WHO DO YOU CONSIDER YOUR GREATEST DEVOTEE?

RANTIDEVA.

THAT KING? JUST BECAUSE HE HAS GIVEN UP HIS KINGDOM AND FASTED FOR FORTY-EIGHT DAYS?

* GOD'S GIFT

*CELESTIAL BEING

* EMANCIPATION OF THE SOUL

30

TALES OF NARADA

The route to your roots

TALES OF NARADA

Sage Narada symbolises unqualified devotion to Lord Vishnu, also known as Narayana. He is inseparable from his veena and has the name of Lord Narayana always on his lips. In the Puranic stories, it is Narada who puts the Lord's devotees to test. But when he himself is put to test will the celestial sage emerge victorious?

Script	Illustrations	Editor
Onkar Nath Sharma	P.B.Kavadi	Anant Pai

NARADA CONQUERS TEMPTATION

NARADA WAS A DEVARSHI* WHO WAS ALWAYS TRAVELLING ROUND THE WORLD, OFFERING GUIDANCE TO THE DEVOTEES OF THE LORD.

AFTER HAVING GAINED TRUE KNOWLEDGE FROM HIS FATHER, BRAHMA...

...HE TOOK THE VOW OF CELIBACY.

I SHALL NOT MARRY. I WILL SERVE LORD NARAYANA.+

* CELESTIAL SAGE + VISHNU

KAMA CAME TO THE COLD, BARREN SPOT WHERE NARADA WAS SITTING, DEEP IN MEDITATION.

AS HE SHOT THE FIRST ARROW...

...THE SCENE SUDDENLY CHANGED...

... AND A BEAUTIFUL APSARA* APPEARED BEFORE NARADA.

* CELESTIAL DAMSEL

SHE BEGAN TO DANCE BEFORE HIM.

BUT NARADA'S EYES WERE CLOSED TO HER CHARMS.

O SAGE, OPEN YOUR EYES AND BEHOLD YOUR SLAVE.

BUT NARADA HARDLY HEARD HER.

REALISING, THAT SHE WOULD NEVER SUCCEED IN DISTRACTING THE SAGE, THE APSARA LEFT FOR HER HEAVENLY ABODE.

KAMA HAD TO ACKNOWLEDGE DEFEAT.

YOU ARE A GREAT ASCETIC, O SUPREME SAGE! I HAVE FAILED. I BEG TO BE FORGIVEN FOR MY AUDACITY.

* SEE AMAR CHITRA KATHA NO. 506- SHIVA PARVATI

* THE GODDESS OF FORTUNE, VISHNU'S CONSORT ⊕VISHNU

* ANOTHER NAME FOR VISHNU

THE NEXT MOMENT—

OH! MY LORD!

AH! THERE HE IS! LORD. WHY DID YOU...

BEFORE HE COULD COMPLETE HIS QUESTION, SHRIMATI HAD GARLANDED VISHNU.

SO THAT WAS IT! HE WANTED HER FOR HIMSELF. THE TRAITOR!

HE CHARGED FORWARD IN A RAGE.

YOU PROMISED TO GIVE ME YOUR FACE AND GAVE ME A MONKEY'S INSTEAD! WHY?

MY DEAR NARADA, YOU ARE A SCHOLAR OF SANSKRIT. DON'T YOU KNOW, HARI ALSO MEANS MONKEY? YOU DIDN'T SPECIFY WHICH HARI YOU MEANT.

* UNLEAVENED BREAD

AND NARADA SET OFF.

I MUST BE CAUTIOUS LEST THE OIL SHOULD SPILL.

AH! AH! THAT WAS A CLOSE CALL! HAD I SLIPPED, THE OIL WOULD HAVE SPILT. I MUST BE MORE CAREFUL.

WHEN NARADA SUCCESSFULLY COMPLETED THE ROUND—

YOU'RE BACK. GOOD! BUT TELL ME HOW MANY TIMES DID YOU REMEMBER ME DURING THE WALK?

NOT ONCE, I'M AFRAID. HOW COULD I? ALL MY ATTENTION WAS FIXED ON THE OIL AND THE VESSEL!

THAT FARMER HAS HARD WORK TO DO. YET HE REMEMBERS ME — AT LEAST A FEW TIMES. WHILE YOU COULD NOT REMEMBER ME EVEN ONCE!

I CONCEDE IT, MY LORD. THOSE WHO REMEMBER YOU AMIDST WORLDLY CARES ARE WITHOUT DOUBT YOUR GREATEST DEVOTEES.

NARADA ENLIGHTENED

THE CELESTIAL SAGE, NARADA, ONCE CAME TO DWARAKA, TO SEE LORD KRISHNA.

WELCOME, NARADA. WHAT BRINGS YOU HERE?

KRISHNA, I WANT TO KNOW WHAT MAYA* IS? CAN YOU EXPLAIN?

NARADA, MAYA CAN'T BE EXPLAINED. IT HAS TO BE EXPERIENCED, TO BE UNDERSTOOD. COME WITH ME.

BOTH KRISHNA AND NARADA LEFT DWARAKA...

* ILLUSION